Our children - our future.

Copyright 2018 by Amanda Clark - All rights reserved.

No part of this publication or the information in it may be quoted from or reproduced in any form by means such as printing, scanning, photocopying or otherwise without prior written permission of the copyright holder. Disclaimer and Terms of Use: Effort has been made to ensure that the information in this book is accurate and complete, however, the author and the publisher do not warrant the accuracy of the information, text and graphics contained within the book due to the rapidly changing nature of science, research, known and unknown facts and internet. The Author and the publisher do not hold any responsibility for errors, omissions or contrary interpretation of the subject matter herein. This book is presented solely for motivational and informational purposes only.

Amanda Clark

Children have two currencies for love: time and attention. When parents invest time and care into their children's emotional bank account, their children grow to know themselves as significant and valuable.

Amanda Clark - an author who helps you to spend time, investing both in kids and yourself.

«As a mother of two, I know it can be hard to get children to read. So you should give them exactly what they want to read! My kids - are my "proofreaders" so I am sure that your angels will read this book with great pleasure.»
- Amanda Clark.

If you are looking for amazing books, join our big family NOW!

https://www.facebook.com/amandakidsauthor/

It was a day like any other
knee deep in toys scattered all around
When he heard the call from his mother
his cheerful smile turned to a frown.

Too much was still left undone that day
as the soldiers stood in his defense
And Leo the lion blocked the way
from the enemies behind the fence.

Made of blocks and keeping them at bay
the dinosaurs unable to chase
All he wanted to do was to play
and she wanted his toys in their place.

"Time to clean your room and have a snack,"
his mother called out from the doorway.
But the toys he did not want to pack
as he would, no doubt, return to play.

"I am not done with them yet today,"
Jonny whined as he turned to his mom.
"So why should I put my toys away?"
he wondered, his voice remaining calm.

"Our belongings we must show respect,
by cleaning them up when we are done.
There is a chance that they could get wrecked
when you return to them for more fun."

As she walked away, he sighed softly
glancing around at all of his toys.
How could he clean up his things promptly
without him making way too much noise?

Just then a thought came into his head
and a plan quickly formed in his mind.
He planned to push them beneath his bed
but was stopped by a voice from behind.

"Treating your toys like that is not fair,
and to do so would be impolite.
In the dark, they would get quite a scare
being packed there together so tight."

Spinning around, he could not believe
even though he saw with his own eyes.
He rubbed them, but still, he did not leave.
This talking train caught him by surprise.

"Your toys called for me to come and help,
fearing to be left beneath your bed.
"It is not kind to do, my young whelp,
I am here to show you how instead.

"Each one of your toys has their own place,
and in that place, they must be returned.
"Every book a spot on the bookcase
until next time their pages are turned.

"The blocks, all red, yellow, green, and blue,
should be put away into their sack.
"The hammer, nails, screwdriver, and screw
must be returned to their plastic rack.

"Leo the lion, the tiger Tim,
and every single one of their friends,
will soon start looking tired and grim
if they are not returned to their pens.

"All the soldiers standing proud and true,
the robots and the dinosaurs too,
they are now tired from playing with you
and must be returned to their own crew.

"Only once they have all been replaced,
each back into their own special spot,
with no chance of them being misplaced
will your toys no longer feel distraught."

Even as the train began to speak
Jonny was shocked to see all his toys,
none of them even trying to sneak,
make their way to the train with no noise.

One after another they all jumped
up into all the empty railcars.
Leaving poor Jonny completely stumped
and feeling like he was seeing stars

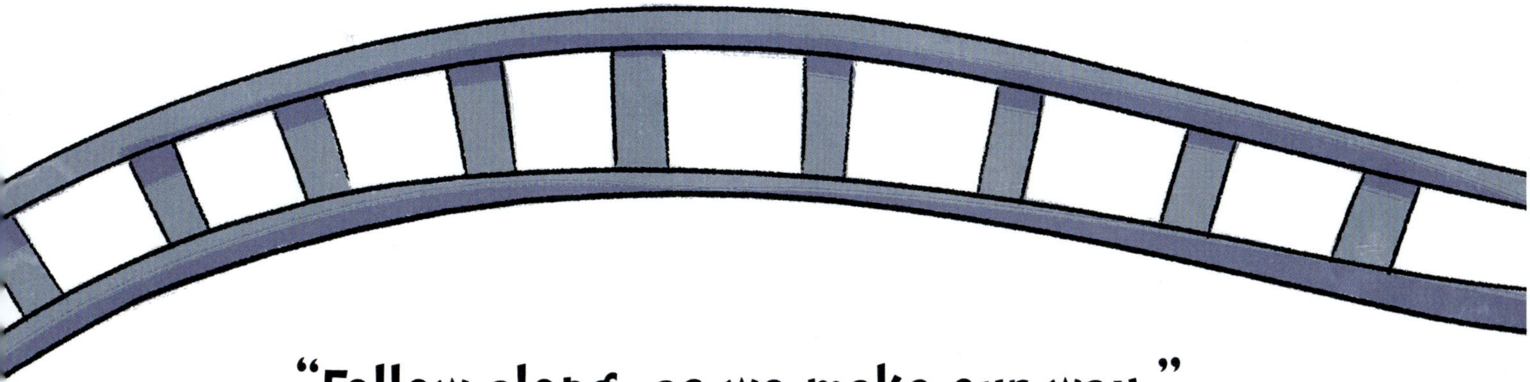

"Follow along, as we make our way,"
the train called out with a quick, "Choo choo."
So surprised, he didn't know what to say
but right then, he knew what he should do.

All over the room, the train led him,
stopping before each one of their homes.
First jumped out Leo the lion and Tim
and after them came the little gnomes.

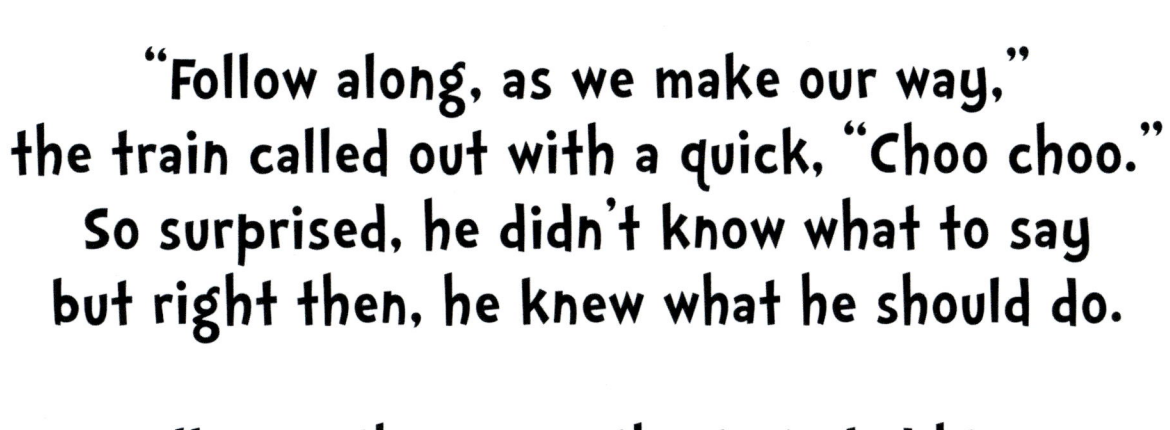

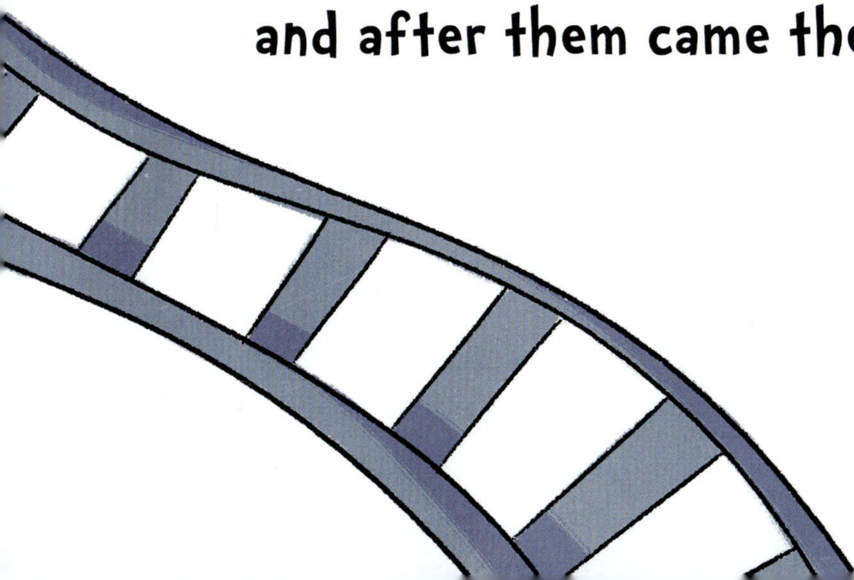

The soldiers and the dinosaurs too,
the robots and the big bag of blocks,
disembarked as the train whistle blew
following their guide; a train that talks.

Once the last of his toys had returned,
each one now in their own special spot,
Jonny smiled at all he had learned
cleaning had made more sense than he thought.

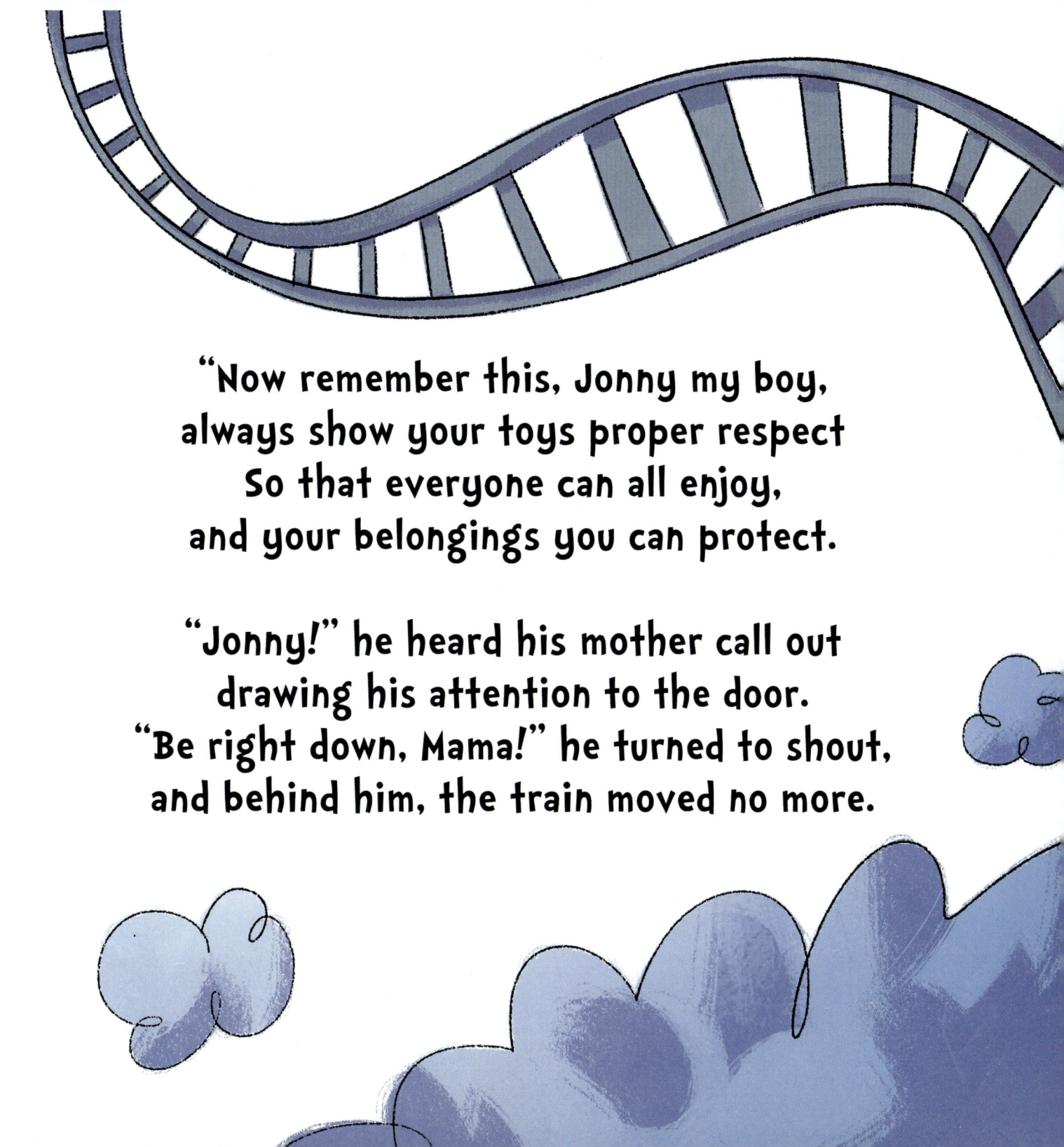

"Now remember this, Jonny my boy,
always show your toys proper respect
So that everyone can all enjoy,
and your belongings you can protect.

"Jonny!" he heard his mother call out
drawing his attention to the door.
"Be right down, Mama!" he turned to shout,
and behind him, the train moved no more.

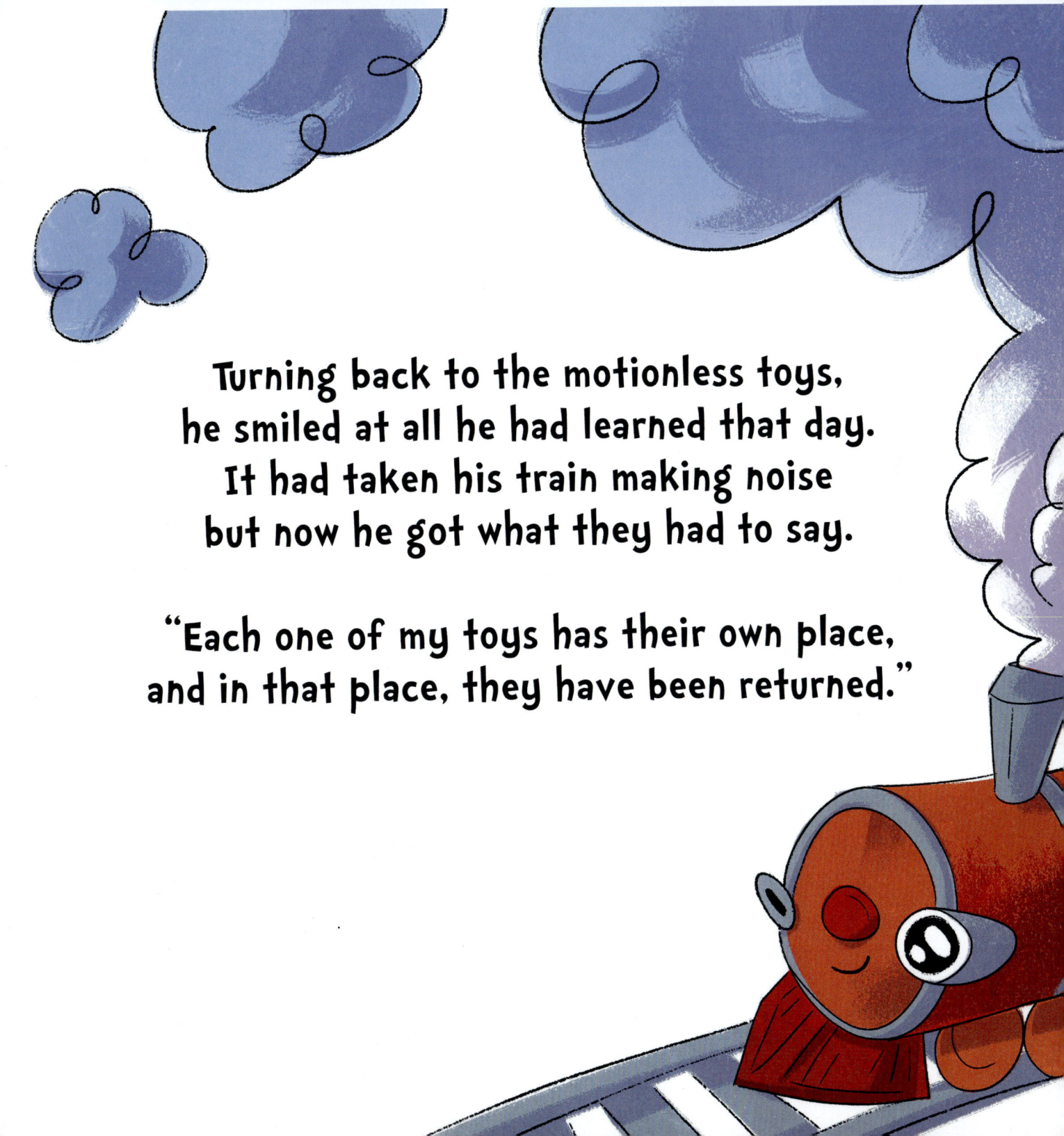

Turning back to the motionless toys,
he smiled at all he had learned that day.
It had taken his train making noise
but now he got what they had to say.

"Each one of my toys has their own place,
and in that place, they have been returned."

«Please, leave a review on amazon.com, if you enjoy this book. Your feedback is very important for me. Thank you.»

Kindly,

Amanda Clark

Made in the USA
Columbia, SC
23 January 2019